Supporting Children with
Down's Syndrome

Hull Learning Services

 **David Fulton** Publishers

1-9-2007
LAN
$19

David Fulton Publishers Ltd
The Chiswick Centre, 414 Chiswick High Road, London W4 5TF

www.fultonpublishers.co.uk

First published in Great Britain by Hull Learning Services

David Fulton Publishers is a division of Granada Learning, part of ITV plc.

Copyright © David Fulton Publishers Ltd 2004

British Library Cataloguing in Publication Data
A catalogue record for this book is available from the British Library.

ISBN 1 84312 221 9

Typeset by Matrix Creative, Wokingham
Printed and bound in Great Britain

ii

Contents

Foreword

This book was produced in partnership with the following services based in Hull, the Special Educational Needs Support Service, the City Educational Psychological Service and the Hull and District Down's Syndrome Association.
It was written by:

Susan Miller: City Educational Psychological Service
Elizabeth Morling: (SENSS)
Susan Wong: Hull and District Down's Syndrome Association.

With grateful thanks to the UK Education Consortium for Children with Down's Syndrome:

Sandy Alton

Jane Beadman

Bob Black

Stephanie Lorenz

Cecilie McKinnon

It is one of a series of eleven titles providing an up-to-date overview of special educational needs for SENCOs, teachers and other professionals and parents.

The books were produced in response to training and information needs raised by teachers, support staff and parents in Hull. The aim of these books is to raise awareness and address many of the issues involved in creating inclusive environments.

We would like to thank senior adviser John Hill for his support and encouragement throughout the development of this series.

For details of other titles and how to order, please go to: www.fultonpublishers.co.uk, or telephone: 0500 618052.

Introduction

Inclusion in education

Inclusion can be demonstrated in a number of ways.

- It recognises that all pupils have different abilities and experiences and seeks to value and gain from these differences. It is not about expecting or trying to make everyone the same or behave in the same way.

- Education involves the process of increasing the participation of students in and reducing their exclusion from the cultures, curricula and communities of local schools.

- It involves restructuring the cultures, policies and practices in schools so that they respond to the diversity of students in their locality.

- It is concerned with the learning and participation of all students vulnerable to exclusionary pressures, not only those with impairments or those who are categorised as having 'special educational needs'.

- It views diversity not as a problem to overcome but as a rich resource to support the learning of all.

The United Nations makes the following distinctions between the definitions of handicap and disability:

Handicap: "A function of the relationship between disabled persons and their environment.... Handicap is the loss or limitation of opportunities to take part in the life of the community on an equal level with others."

Disability: "Any restriction or lack (resulting from an impairment) of ability to perform an activity in the manner or within the range considered normal for a human being."

"Disabled persons have the inherent right to respect for their human dignity. Disabled persons, whatever the origin, nature and seriousness of their handicaps and disabilities, have the same fundamental rights as their fellow citizens of the same age, which implies first and foremost the right to enjoy a decent life, as normal and as full as possible."

"Disabled persons are entitled to the measures designed to enable them to become as self reliant as possible."

(The United Nations Declaration of Human Rights of Disabled People (1975))

"Education is vital to the creation of a fully inclusive society, a society in which all members see themselves as valued for the contribution they make. We owe all children – whatever their particular needs and circumstance – the opportunity to develop to their full potential to contribute economically and to play a full part as active citizens."

(David Blunkett, former Secretary of State for Education and Employment)

Implications of the Disability Discrimination Act (1995) as amended by the SEN and Disability Act 2001

Part one of the Act:

- strengthens the right of children to be educated in mainstream schools;
- requires LEAs to arrange for parents and/or children with SEN to be provided with advice on SEN matters and also a means of settling disputes with schools and LEAs (parent partnership services and mediation/conciliation schemes);
- requires schools to tell parents where they are making special educational provision for their child and allows schools to request a statutory assessment of a pupil's needs.

In accordance with the above Act:

LEAs and schools must:

- not treat disabled pupils less favourably;
- make reasonable adjustments so that the physical, sensory and learning needs of disabled pupils are accommodated in order that they are not put at a substantial disadvantage to pupils who are not disabled.
- plan strategically and make progress in increasing not only physical accessibility to the school's premises and to the curriculum but also to improve the delivery of written information in an accessible way to disabled pupils (i.e. access to the curriculum via oral means, as well as the written word).

Definition of disability

- The Disability Discrimination Act uses a very broad definition of 'disability'. A person has a disability if he or she has a physical or mental impairment that has a substantial and long-term adverse effect on his or her ability to carry out normal day-to-day activities.
- The DDA definition of disability covers physical disabilities, sensory impairments such as those affecting sight or hearing and learning difficulties.

The role of the governing body

The Code of Practice states that 'the governing body of a community, voluntary or foundation school' must:

- do its best to ensure that the necessary provision is made for any pupil who has special educational needs

- ensure that, where the 'responsible person' - the head teacher or the appropriate governor – has been informed by the LEA that a pupil has special educational needs, those needs are made known to all who are likely to teach them

- ensure that teachers in the school are aware of the importance of identifying, and providing for, those pupils who have special educational needs

- consult the LEA and the governing bodies of other schools, when it seems to be necessary or desirable in the interests of co-ordinated special educational provision in the area as a whole

- ensure that a pupil with special educational needs joins in the activities of the school together with pupils who do not have special educational needs, so far as is reasonably practical and compatible with the child receiving the special educational provision their learning needs call for and the efficient education of the pupils with whom they are educated and the efficient use of resources

- report to parents of the implication of the school's policy for pupils with special educational needs

See section 317, Education Act 1996:

- have regard to this Code of Practice when carrying out its duties toward all pupils with special educational needs

See Section 313, Education Act 1996:

- ensure that parents are notified of a decision by the school that SEN provision is being made for their child.

Including the pupil with Down's syndrome

Education for all pupils should be a positive experience. Pupils with Down's syndrome succeed in mainstream schools for a number of reasons.

- Research shows that pupils do better academically when working in inclusive settings.
- Daily opportunities to mix with typically developing peers provides models for normal and age-appropriate behaviour.
- Pupils have opportunities to develop relationships with pupils from their own community.
- Attending mainstream school is a key step towards inclusion in the life of the community and society as a whole.
- Successful inclusion is a key step towards preparing pupils with special educational needs to become full and contributing members of the community, and society as a whole.
- Other pupils gain an understanding about disability, tolerance and how to care for and support other pupils with special needs. As David Blunkett writes in his Foreword to the 1997 Green Paper, "[where] all children are included as equal partners in the school community the benefits are felt by all."

Factors for inclusion to succeed:

- the determination to make it a positive experience;
- the attitude of the whole school should reflect this;
- a positive attitude solves problems;
- schools require a clear and sensitive policy on inclusion;
- senior management should support their staff and provide training to develop their skills to meet the needs of their pupils.

Characteristics

Down's syndrome is one of the most common forms of learning disability: about 1 in every 1000 live births a year. It is caused by the presence of an extra copy of chromosome 21. Instead of the usual 46 chromosomes, a person with Down's syndrome has 47.

An overview of characteristics of pupils with Down's syndrome

- There is **some degree of learning difficulty** from mild to severe.

- **Environmental factors** play an important part in development as well as genetic factors.

- **Pupils vary** as widely in their development and progress as typically developing pupils.

- Pupils with Down's syndrome **develop more slowly than their peers**, arriving at each stage of development at a later age and staying there for longer. The developmental gap between pupils with Down's syndrome and their peers may widen with age.

- Their skills **can continue to develop** through life.

Possible medical problems

There are certain medical problems which are more prevalent in pupils with Down's syndrome. However, they are not unique to those with Down's syndrome and also appear in the rest of the population.

The problems may include:

- 40–50% of those born with Down's syndrome have heart problems, half of which require heart surgery;

- a significant number of pupils with Down's syndrome have hearing and visual problems;

- some pupils have a thyroid disorder;

- pupils may have a poor immune system;

- some pupils have respiratory problems, frequent coughs and colds;

- some pupils may experience obstruction of the gastrointestinal tract.

Most of these problems are treatable with advancing medical care. The Down's Syndrome Association together with the Down's Syndrome Medical Interest Group have produced health care guidelines to assist families and health professionals to set up screening programmes. This enables health problems to be identified at an early stage and treated before they become more serious. School staff should seek information from parents/carers, specialist advice from Down's paediatric nurses or the school medical service and the Down's Syndrome Association.

N.B. Some pupils may not experience any health difficulties.

Supporting pupils with Down's syndrome

Pupils with Down's syndrome are not just generally delayed in their development, they also have a specific learning profile with characteristic strengths and weaknesses. These characteristics, in conjunction with individual needs and variations within that profile, need to be considered.

Factors that may facilitate learning for pupils with Down's syndrome:

Strong visual awareness and visual learning skills include:

- the ability to learn and use sign, gesture and visual support;
- the ability to learn and use the written word;
- the ability to model the behaviour and attitudes of peers and adults;
- the ability to learn using practical curriculum material and hands-on activities.

Factors that may inhibit learning for pupils with Down's syndrome:

- limited cognitive functioning;
- delayed fine and gross motor skills;
- auditory and visual impairment;
- speech and language impairment;
- short-term auditory memory deficit;
- shorter concentration span;
- difficulties with consolidation and retention;
- difficulties with generalisation and reasoning;
- sequencing difficulties;
- avoidance strategies.

Many of the following strategies to support pupils with Down's syndrome will be recognisable as good teaching practice and so will be equally suitable for other pupils in school.

Classroom practice

The pupil with Down's syndrome should be treated as an individual, as a personality in his/her own right. Normal good practice is appropriate for these pupils. However, it may be relevant to make certain considerations.

- Consider the pupil's level of learning development.
- Have expectations for behaviour as for any other pupil.
- Consider the use of classroom assistants to support the pupil with Down's syndrome when whole class teaching is taking place, as delayed language skills may limit the pupil's access to the teacher's input and instructions.
- Provide visual input for the pupil in the above situation, e.g. cue cards, concrete objects, demonstrations of tasks to be done.
- Be aware that the classroom environment can inhibit access for those with short stature, i.e. furniture, equipment, handles that are too high or too large.
- Ensure that equipment meets the pupil's stage of development.
- Encourage co-operative working with more able peers, being aware that the pupil with Down's syndrome has a lot to contribute.
- Place the pupil with articulate peers to give good models.
- Consider when the pupil should work in a whole-class situation, in a small group or in a one-to-one situation.
- Inform all school staff of the expectations for the pupil, e.g. lunchtime supervisors, parent helpers, to ensure consistency for the pupil, which will prevent 'babying' or inappropriate behaviour occurring.
- Ensure that information about the pupil is conveyed to all staff that have contact with the pupil.
- Pass on all information about the pupil, at end-of-year changes, including strategies which succeed, to capitalise and build on good practice.
- Give the pupil with Down's syndrome the same amount of teacher input as other pupils.
- Give praise for tasks that are successfully completed.
- Acknowledge the level of effort required to achieve a task.

Differentiation

Pupils with Down's syndrome may need their work differentiated in order for them to access the curriculum.

There are a number of ways in which differentiation can take place:

- Take into account the learning profile of the pupil with Down's syndrome and the factors within it, which will have physical and cognitive implications.
- A minority of pupils with very specific needs may require a curriculum, which is reduced in its breadth to enable a focus on their specific learning needs.
- Provide work at the appropriate stage of development.
- Use publications to find the appropriate level of work, e.g.
  - 'Kingston upon Hull Target Setting' book;
  - 'Curriculum Guidelines' (QCA) for pupils unlikely to achieve above level 2 at key stage 4;
  - 'Supporting the Target Setting Process' (DfEE);
  - 'Including all children in the Literacy Hour and Daily Mathematics Lesson' (DfES).
- Use descriptors for previous key stages.
- Have regard to IEP targets when planning work.
- Break skills down into small steps (see Appendices 3 and 4).
- Use concrete objects to support work when other pupils may be working in the abstract.
- Give small tasks, which are appropriate to the pupil's level of concentration.
- Ensure equipment is appropriate to the pupil's level of development.
- Give support in practical sessions where manipulation of equipment may be difficult, e.g. number fans in the Numeracy Strategy, science equipment.
- Allow time for planning and liaison between staff to prepare and differentiate materials.

Visual impairment

Many pupils with Down's syndrome have some sort of visual impairment: 60–70% being prescribed glasses before the age of seven.

Strategies to support the pupil:

- place the pupil near the front of the class;
- ensure that the pupil can see the whiteboard, big book in Literacy Hour;
- use larger bold type;
- use simple, clear presentation in worksheets, with appropriately sized font;
- ensure print size in reading books is of an appropriate size;
- consider the use of larger squared paper in mathematics;
- use heavy black lines for line guides;
- give pens with wider nibs, which produce lines that are easier to see;
- ensure that the pupil wears spectacles if prescribed;
- use appropriate material when the pupil is being assessed, e.g. QCA material;
- seek advice from the specialist visual impairment service involved with the pupil.

Hearing impairment

Many pupils with Down's syndrome experience some hearing loss especially in the early years. Levels of hearing can vary from day to day. It is necessary to determine whether hearing difficulties or poor understanding of language cause a lack of response.

Strategies to support hearing difficulties:

- place the pupil near the front of the class;
- face the pupil when speaking to him/her;
- gain the pupil's attention before speaking;
- reinforce speech with signs, gestures and encouragement to watch other pupils;
- give other prompts – pictures, prompts in a written form;
- repeat other pupils' responses, e.g. in the Literacy Hour;
- the teacher should repeat instructions to the pupil after the whole group input, to ensure understanding;
- ask the pupil to repeat what is to be done;
- seek advice from the hearing impairment service, if appropriate.

Adult support for the pupil

Pupils with Down's syndrome may require some level of additional adult support to cover the following areas:

- encouraging a growing level of independence;
- developing language skills;
  - signing (if necessary);
  - implementing a speech and language programme devised by a speech and language therapist;
  - promoting good listening skills;
- developing confidence;
- developing self-esteem;
- developing social interaction;
- developing co-operative working;
- developing self-help skills;
  - hygiene;
  - dressing;
  - independent movement around the site;
- supporting access to the curriculum;
  - delivering differentiated material devised by the teacher;
  - making additional materials;
  - simplifying instructions;
  - providing visual clues;
  - providing alternative recording methods.

Support staff: effective deployment

Not all pupils with Down's syndrome will require additional adult support in order to meet their needs within the classroom. For those pupils who have a more significant level of need, however, the provision of support staff is vital to ensure that their needs can be met.

Teachers may consider the following issues to ensure the most effective deployment of support staff:

- Support staff should promote independence at all times.
- It will not be necessary to work alongside the pupil in every lesson.
- Consider the position of support staff within the classroom.
- Allow the pupil to focus on the teacher, rather than on support staff.
- Support staff should take notes during teacher input in order to reinforce key points at a later stage in the lesson.
- Support staff should monitor and record appropriate information about the pupil, e.g. work output, temperament.
- Liaison procedures between home and school should be established under the guidance of the SENCO/Head of Year/class teacher or form tutor.
- Support staff should work under the direction of the SENCO, class teacher or individual subject teachers.
- In practical sessions when the pupil needs to manipulate specialised equipment, support staff should work under the direction of the pupil.
- Withdrawal of the pupil for programmes, such as speech and language therapy, should be negotiated with the SENCO and individual subject teachers.

Recognise that the ultimate responsibility for a pupil's access to the curriculum is that of the classroom teacher. Support staff facilitate the delivery of an appropriately differentiated curriculum under the direction of the teacher.

Support staff: roles and responsibilities

Support staff should:

Have a clear understanding of their roles and responsibilities:

- have a knowledge of their job description;
- maintain a professional demeanour with parents;
- be aware of school policies with regard to behaviour, anti-bullying, child protection;
- respect the confidentiality of information for all pupils.

Be aware of channels of communication within the school:

- ensure that information given by parents is given to the appropriate member of staff – class teacher, SENCO;
- ensure that communication with outside agencies is carried out in consultation with the SENCO;
- ensure that recommendations and reports from outside agencies are passed to the teacher and SENCO;
- ensure that information given to parents is with the knowledge of the class teacher;
- ensure that there is a mechanism for disseminating information to support staff about school activities, e.g. daily diary, staff room notice board.

Be recognised as valued members of a team:

- participate in the planning and monitoring process.

Be encouraged to make use of their personal skills:

- share skills, e.g. ICT, creative skills.

Be supported with appropriate on-going professional development:

- observe and learn from other professionals in school and in other establishments;
- undertake training in school and through external courses.

Encourage the pupil's independence at all times:

- promote independent work habits;
- promote independent life skills;
- promote independent play skills.

Support staff: guidelines for working with pupils

Avoid	but instead …
sitting next to the pupil at all times	work with other pupils, whilst keeping an eye on the pupil you are assigned to
offering too close an oversight during breaks and lunchtimes	encourage playing with peers, introduce games to include others if necessary
collecting equipment for the pupil or putting it away	encourage the pupil to carry this out with independence
completing a task for a pupil	ensure that work is at an appropriate level and is carried out with minimal support (note any support given)
allowing behaviour which is not age-appropriate to the pupil, e.g. holding hands in the playground or in school	encourage the development of more age-appropriate peer relationships by social engineering, 'buddying ' or circle of friends
making unnecessary allowances for the pupil	ensure that school rules apply
preventing the pupil from taking the consequences of their actions	insist that the pupil takes the responsibility for and the consequences of his/her actions
tolerating bad behaviour	follow the behaviour policy
making unrealistic demands on the pupil	ensure instructions and work are at the appropriate level
making decisions for the pupil	give the pupil opportunities to make choices and decisions
over-dependency on the support assistant	encourage independent behaviour and work.

Developing speech and language

Pupils with Down's syndrome typically have a speech and language impairment. The language delay is caused by a combination of factors, some of which are physical and some due more to perceptual and cognitive problems. Any delay in learning to understand and use language is likely to lead to cognitive delay. The level of knowledge and understanding and thus the ability to access the curriculum will inevitably be affected.

The consequences of a delay in language acquisition may result in:

- a smaller vocabulary, which can lessen the ability to acquire general knowledge;
- difficulty learning the rules of grammar;
- the omission of connecting words, prepositions;
- the ability to learn new vocabulary more easily than the rules of grammar;
- problems in learning and managing social language;
- problems in understanding specific language of the curriculum;
- difficulty in understanding instructions and consequently following instructions;
- receptive skills generally being greater than expressive skills;
- difficulty in physically forming words because of a smaller mouth cavity and weaker mouth and tongue muscles;
- fewer opportunities to engage in language and conversation which hampers the development of language;
- difficulty in asking for information or help;
- adults who answer for them or finish their sentences;
- insufficient practice to improve their clarity of speech.

There are a number of strategies to support the development of speech and language skills:

- Give the pupil time to process language and respond.
- Listen carefully to the pupil; understanding of unclear speech improves with familiarity.
- Ensure face-to-face interaction and good eye contact with the pupil.
- Use simple and familiar language and short, concise sentences.
- Check the pupil's understanding of instructions by asking him/her to repeat the instructions.
- Avoid ambiguous vocabulary which can cause confusion.
- Reinforce speech with facial expression, gesture and sign.
- Teach reading from an early stage and use the printed word to support limited speech and language.
- Reinforce spoken instructions with print, pictures, diagrams, symbols and concrete materials.
- Emphasise key words, reinforcing in a visual manner.
- Teach grammar through print – flashcards, games, pictures of prepositions and symbols.
- Avoid closed questions and encourage the pupil to speak in more than one-word utterances.
- Encourage the pupil to speak aloud in class by providing visual prompts. The pupil may find it easier to read information than to speak spontaneously.
- Use a home-school diary to prompt the pupil when telling his/her 'news' and help adults to understand what the pupil is saying.
- Develop language through drama and role-play.
- Set up regular and additional opportunities to speak to others, e.g. taking and reading messages.
- Provide lots of short listening activities/games to strengthen auditory skills.
- Use visual means, e.g. prompt cards to promote good sitting and listening skills.
- Place the pupil near the teacher; allow him/her to hold an object to aid concentration.
- Provide means of supporting the understanding of teacher-input by translating into more visual means, e.g. use of a small white board, handling objects.
- Use visual and tactile materials to reinforce oral work.
- Use Makaton (or some alternative) to support communication, encourage the use of signing by the whole class.

Addressing behaviour issues

As with other pupils, those with Down's syndrome may display behaviour problems and may need to be taught to behave in a socially acceptable way and to respond in an appropriate manner. Pupils with Down's syndrome may find the environment around them a little confusing: they may need additional support and may take longer to develop appropriate behaviour.

There are some basic expectations in schools that pupils are required to follow, which may need to be taught explicitly:

- an awareness of expected behaviour at certain times, e.g. lining up, sitting appropriately in assembly;
- class and school rules;
- appropriate responses to requests and instructions;
- co-operation with others at work and play.

It may be necessary to develop strategies to address behavioural issues, which may arise:

- Ensure that the pupil is aware of the expectations or rules of a given situation.
- Ensure all staff know that the pupil with Down's syndrome must be disciplined as any other pupil.
- Use short, clear instructions appropriate to the pupil's level of understanding and support, with demonstrations of the task.
- Distinguish the 'can't do' from the 'won't do'.
- Develop a range of strategies to deal with avoidance behaviours.
- Ensure work is at the appropriate level.
- Match the length of the task to the pupil's ability to concentrate.
- Encourage positive behaviour by developing good behaviour prompt pictures, e.g. tidying up or sitting appropriately.
- Reinforce the desired behaviour immediately with visual, oral or tangible rewards. Cumulative rewards, e.g. golden time given at the end of the week, has little meaning to a pupil with short-term memory problems.
- Any penalties or punishments should take place straight after the event and not some time later.
- Ignore attention-seeking behaviour, within reasonable limits.

- Dealing with inappropriate behaviour should be a shared responsibility, not just the role of the support assistant.

- Ensure that the pupil works with peers who can act as good role models.

- Teach new rules which apply to new situations in a very explicit way, as the pupil moves through school.

- Avoid assuming that difficulties are lodged within the pupil or are specific to Down's syndrome.

- Seek support from outside agencies, if behaviour problems cannot be addressed through school intervention.

Developing memory

Pupils with Down's syndrome experience poor auditory short-term memory and auditory processing skills.

> The auditory short-term memory is the memory store used to hold, process, understand and assimilate spoken language long enough to respond to it. Any deficit in short-term auditory memory will greatly affect pupils' ability to respond to the spoken word or learn from any situation entirely reliant on their auditory skills. In addition, they will find it more difficult to follow and remember verbal instructions.

There are a variety of ways of improving memory skills:

- Sing nursery rhymes frequently, leave a pause and let the pupil give the last word e.g. 'Humpty Dumpty sat on the …'
- Read simple stories with repetitive lines, e.g. 'the Gingerbread Man' and ask the pupil to join in the repetitions.
- Read a very simple story a few times and at strategic points ask what comes next.
- Tell jokes and silly poems, which the pupil can take home to relate to their family.
- Use chants, raps and rhymes to learn alphabetical order, days of the week, etc.
- Ask the pupil to fetch an article, build up the number of articles to be fetched over time.
- Ask the pupil to put equipment away in the correct place.
- Play 'Kim's Game' with two articles on the tray, initially, gradually increasing the number of articles.
- Talk about what is being done when a task is being carried out, e.g. during baking. Recall what has been done by asking simple questions using the equipment, e.g. 'What did we put in the bowl?'
- Ask the pupil to repeat what she/he has to do when instructions have been given.
- Give opportunities to take messages.

Encourage coping strategies to overcome poor memory:

- Develop the use of cue cards, e.g. a picture which shows what is to be done, in order to supplement poor auditory memory.
- Utilise notebooks, visual timetables, homework notebooks, home-school diaries.
- Use appropriate computer software to help develop skills.

Where possible always accompany auditory information with visual cues, modelling and practical examples.

Developing mathematical skills

Pupils with Down's syndrome will probably experience difficulty in this area of the curriculum because:

- poor auditory memory causes difficulty in remembering instructions;
- development of limited language skills may affect concept development;
- sensory impairments affect access;
- acquisition of abstract concepts may be restricted;
- poor fine motor skills may inhibit recording.

It will be necessary to support the development of mathematics through a number of strategies:

- Develop a structure within the Numeracy Strategy which encompasses a small-steps approach – 'Mathsteps' (LDA) may provide an assessment and a programme.
- Consider alternatives to mental maths.
- Give direct teaching of component skills (it will not happen incidentally).
- Give opportunities for daily repetition of what has been learnt.
- Give lots of practice to consolidate learning at each stage.
- Use precise, consistent language.
- Give attention to learning mathematical vocabulary: LDA's 'Talking Maths' photographs can be helpful.
- Give a verbal description to the pupil of what is being learnt.
- Learning needs to be practical and experiential in the class, e.g. cubes, number lines, coins.
- Skills which have been learnt, need to be generalised to other settings.
- Give instructions in a multi-sensory manner.
- Consider the use of alternative methods of recording answers to prevent poor motor skills hindering progress, e.g. an adult to scribe, the use of stickers with pre-written numbers, number stamps.
- Provide simplified, uncluttered worksheets.
- Provide a small-steps approach to ensure success.
- Consider use of ICT, e.g. Number shark, Talking maths books, Number tiles to provide means of consolidating concepts.

Developing reading skills

Pupils with Down's syndrome can become good readers, with the ability to learn to read with meaning. Reading can:

- improve language skills;
- develop the ability to think and reason;
- aid understanding;
- improve access to a variety of areas of the curriculum;
- overcome difficulties in taking understanding from the spoken language.

A number of considerations need to be taken into account in order to develop reading skills:

- It is not necessary to be 'ready to read', particularly for the pupil with poor expressive language – start sooner rather than later.

- Some pupils may come to school with some vocabulary or with a high level of skills, which can be built upon.

- Use a whole word approach to build up sight vocabulary.

- Teach words initially which are relevant to the pupil, e.g. mum, dad, cat and dog, which could be linked to photographs to make the pupil's first book.

- Use a structured reading scheme, e.g. 'PM Starters' which gradually introduces high frequency words.

- Supplement commercial schemes with a customised reading scheme, to provide a very structured approach, which could be linked to the pupil's interest.

- Generalise words learnt to other situations, e.g. look for words in the environment, attach notes to objects with familiar words for the pupil to read, e.g. this is John's book.

- Differentiate work in the Literacy Hour. Phonic skills may be difficult to acquire because accurate hearing, discrimination of sounds and problem solving skills are required.

- Develop a phonic programme alongside the whole word approach, e.g. Jolly phonics scheme.

- Consider an alternative to speech, e.g. the pupil signs the words so that the development of reading can progress.

- Give the pupil time to think before prompting.

- Recognise that overlearning will be necessary to consolidate skills that have been learnt.

Developing independent writing

Pupils with Down's syndrome may take longer to develop independent writing skills because of difficulties with:

- short-term auditory memory;
- speech and language skills;
- fine motor skills;
- organising and sequencing information;
- sequencing events;
- sequencing words into a sentence.

Pupils with Down's syndrome can be supported to develop independent writing skills in a number of ways:

- Provide sequencing activities, e.g. sequencing cards showing activities during the day.
- Capitalise on reading skills by using a word bank and a sentence stand to build sentences.
- Provide visual prompts to develop independence:
  - flash cards;
  - picture cues to support the structure of a story;
  - sentence starts on cards, for the pupil to copy and finish; Here is a …, I can see the …;
  - desk top charts with everyday words; colours, days of the week;
  - key word prompts to support story writing.
- Encourage verbal rehearsal of a sentence before it is written.
- Refer to the home/school diary to help the pupil recall familiar events to write about.
- Provide concrete experiences to discuss and describe in his/her writing.
- Encourage the use of cursive script to aid fluency.
- Provide alternative methods of recording the pupil's ideas:
  - scribe;
  - cloze procedure;
  - a series of pictures to tell a story, e.g. from a visit, accompanied by captions, written by the pupil or adult;
  - record on tape the pupil recounting his/her story, which can then be transcribed by an adult;

- use of a word processor (teach keyboard skills);
- use of computers with specialist software, e.g. Clicker 4, computer programs, e. g. Ready for writing, voice activated computers, Widget 'Writing with Symbols' program, which links symbols and words:

I can jump

I can read

I can draw

Teaching spelling

Pupils with Down's syndrome will learn to spell mainly from visual memory. Delayed speech and language skills, limited vocabulary and poor auditory memory may cause difficulties when learning to spell words.

A number of suggestions need to be taken into account to help with the acquisition of spellings:

- Ensure that the words being taught are within their understanding.
- Ensure the pupil can read the words to be learnt.
- Be realistic about the number of spellings being taught and revise regularly.
- Teach words which will promote his/her speech and language development.
- Teach words which are required for specific subjects being covered, e.g. to fit a history topic.
- Teach spellings in a visual manner, e.g. look-cover-write-check, finger tracing, writing in sand, magnetic letters.
- Reinforce meanings of abstract words with symbols or signs.
- Provide a word bank with pictures to reinforce meaning, arrange alphabetically.
- Develop a spelling programme, which allows for progress in small steps.
- Explore spelling activities on the computer, e.g. Starspell 2001.
- Teach simple basic word families by clearly explaining the pattern and colour coding similar letter groups/patterns within words.
- Use a spelling partner to test each others words.
- Use picture dictionaries in preference to 'normal' dictionaries.
- Play games to support the learning of spellings, e.g. simple crosswords, word searches.

Fine and gross motor skills

Many pupils with Down's syndrome have poor muscle tone, loose joints, slack ligaments and short stubby fingers, which affect their fine and gross motor skills.

There are a number of strategies which can be implemented, as the pupil progresses, to develop gross and fine motor skills:

- Encourage a wide range of outdoor play at home and school.
- Encourage full participation in all aspects of P.E.
- Give opportunities to develop eye hand co-ordination, e.g. threading appropriately sized beads onto dowelling, plastic coated wires, stiffened laces.
- Provide wrist-strengthening activities, e.g. screw toys, opening screw tops, sharpening pencils.
- Develop finger-strengthening activities, e.g. rolling, tracing, drawing, cutting, squeezing and building.
- Encourage a pincer grip by picking up small items, squeezing spring pegs and using finger puppets.
- Use a wide range of multi-sensory activities and materials, e.g. chalks, felt tip pens, a variety of paper, white boards, using fingers in the sand to trace over writing patterns.
- Develop scissor skills by carrying out activities, e.g. picking up objects with tweezers, tongs, squeezing bottles, using a paper punch and follow a small steps approach (see appendix 4).
- Consider the use of the 'Write from the Start' programme to develop writing and perceptual skills.
- Be aware of the order of skill development; i.e. the pupil should be able to produce certain shapes before handwriting is introduced.
- Use a structured handwriting scheme.
- Ensure furniture is at the correct height for the pupil.
- Specialised or modified equipment may be needed, e.g. short-handled paintbrushes, triangular pencils and pens, spring scissors (Stirex, Nottingham Rehab), inset puzzles with large knobs, appropriate equipment for science, technology.
- Avoid excess copying from the blackboard: select and highlight a small piece to copy or provide a short version on paper to copy.
- Provide alternative recording methods of recording the pupil's ideas.

Developing self-esteem

There are a number of strategies that may help to build self-esteem:

- Make all goals challenging but attainable.
- Set work at the appropriate level for the pupil's development.
- Convey by the adult's manner that the pupil is a valued member of the class.
- Have feedback sessions at the end of a lesson, which include an element of success.
- Make rewards appropriate to the pupil's level of development and straight after the event.
- Reward success, academic or otherwise, with real congratulations and praise (within sensible limits).
- Display the pupil's work alongside other pupil's work.
- Acknowledge the pupil's strengths, e.g. politeness, kindness and perseverance.
- Raise the pupil's status within the group by giving jobs, e.g. being a monitor.
- Give all pupil's the same opportunities.
- Ensure all staff are aware of the pupil's difficulties and support in the appropriate way.
- Ensure that staff share any successful strategies as the pupil moves through the school.
- Encourage the pupil to make contributions to his/her IEP and to be a part of the review process.
- Celebrate the pupil's success with their parents (sharing the same information as with other parents).

Developing self-help skills

The delay in developing self-help skills for the majority of pupils with Down's syndrome will be related to their general delay. It will be relevant to develop some self-help skills within the school setting.

- Co-operation between home and school should be established in order for self-help programmes to achieve success.
- Peers should be used as good role models.
- A small-steps approach should be used to teach skills.
- Backward chaining can be a useful technique, e.g. when teaching a pupil to put on socks:
  1. turn down the top of the sock, place on the pupil's foot and allow the pupil to pull up;
  2. repeat but allow the pupil to pull over the heel;
  3. pull the sock over the toes and the pupil pulls the sock up;
  4. the pupil puts the sock on completely with verbal prompts.
- Dressing-up activities in the house corner, with large clothes, gives opportunities to practise in a fun situation.
- Programmes should be related to 'real' situations, e.g. dressing skills could be practised in PE, playtime, rather than being carried out in isolation.
- Encourage parents to dress their children in, or encourage older children to choose clothes which will allow them to achieve independence, e.g. Velcro™ fastenings, elasticated waists, coats which are easier to put on and fasten up.
- Picture cues can be used to remind pupils of the order, e.g. pictures which show what to do when washing hands, the sequence required to put on clothes after PE.

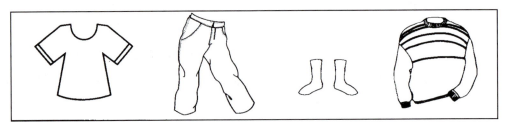

- There is no reason, other than a specific medical one, why a pupil with Down's syndrome should not be toilet trained. The pupil may be delayed in his/her readiness for the process to begin and it may take a longer time to complete. School nurses may give advice. The process should be done in conjunction with the parents.

Promoting peer-group relationships

It may be necessary to consider ways to encourage good relationships between peers, through a variety of methods.

- Encourage staff and pupils to use sign's e.g. Makaton, if this is the pupil's main form of communication.

- Acknowledge that other pupils may be inclined to 'baby' the young pupil with Down's syndrome, which should be discouraged.

- Adults should be sensitive to the pupils need to have 'space' at breaktimes.

- Adults should not be a barrier to the pupil's interaction with others.

- Acknowledge the age of the pupil and allow him/her to be with his/her peers.

- Be aware that speech and language difficulties can be a barrier to developing relationships and that it may be necessary to:
  - encourage play with other pupils;
  - develop understanding of the 'rules' of being a friend;
  - use role-play 'social stories', to teach more age-appropriate play and the unspoken rules of social interaction.

- Organise structured play sessions led by a support assistant in the playground (if necessary), e.g. playing ring games, skipping games, ball games.

- Consider setting up a friendship rota or a 'buddy system' (in a sensitive manner).

- Encourage co-operative learning by working with a partner or in a small group.

- Do not always put the pupil with less able or less well-motivated pupils.

- Pupils with Down's syndrome can benefit from working with more able pupils if their work is suitably differentiated.

- Raise awareness of learning disabilities during circle time.

- Use peer support instead of adult support whenever possible.

- Encourage participation in lunchtime or after-school clubs.

- Encourage self-awareness, identity, self-esteem and self-confidence.

- Recognise that the pupil may need different approaches, e.g. to discipline, but allow other pupils to recognise fair play.

About my school.
I like to play with my
frens. I like hot
dinners. I like to do P.E.
The best thing is
golden time becase
I can make toast.
But I love holedays.
                by Tim wong age 10

Home/school liaison

"Parents hold key information and have a critical role to play in their children's education" (Code of Practice, 2001)

There are a number of considerations, which can be made in order to foster good home/school partnerships:

- Value the information that parents give about their child.
- Parents should be aware of the Code of Practice and its implications for them:
  - have an understanding of the stages within the Code and know at which stage their child is at;
  - should be invited to contribute to IEPs, attend review meetings and discuss how they can support the IEP.
- Provide reports for parents before annual reviews.
- Parents should know whom to contact if they have concerns about their child, for example:
  - class teacher;
  - SENCO;
  - headteacher;
  - special needs governor.
- Parental concerns should be listened to, acknowledged and addressed.
- Involve parents if the pupil is perceived to be having difficulties in school and seek co-operative solutions.
- Encourage parents to become involved in the life of the school, e.g. as reading partners, helpers on school trips or school governors.
- Inform parents of visits from other professionals, e.g. educational psychologist, speech and language therapist and ensure any relevant reports are shared.
- Consult parents when changes in provision are being considered.
- Ensure parents are aware that their child's work is valued, e.g. through including his/her work in displays.
- Use a home/school diary to allow school and home to create a dialogue about the pupil's home and school life, which will overcome restricted language skills.

Transitions

A number of considerations need to made, as the pupil makes the transition from primary to secondary school.

- The choice of a receiving school with a positive attitude.
- A carefully prepared transition plan, which is drawn up at the Annual Review, held in the final year of primary school. This should involve:
  - the teachers, SENCOs and support assistants from the primary school and the secondary school;
  - professionals from outside agencies, e.g. educational psychologists, speech and language therapists, etc;
  - parents.

The plan should consider:
  - visits from secondary school staff to the pupil in the primary school;
  - additional visits to the receiving school;
  - home/school communication;
  - management of support;
  - access to the curriculum;
  - transfer of the pupil's IEP;
  - personal profile of the pupil.

- Staff training should be put into place: about Down's syndrome, the pupil's learning profile, differentiation.
- The appropriate use of adult support (possibly more than one worker) should be discussed, in order to support subjects and promote independence.
- Consideration should be given to the pupil's stamina related to school on large sites – this may require support.
- Support for the pupil to learn new routines, understand new expectations for behaviour, learn the layout of the school and transition from one lesson to another will be necessary.
- Peer group integration may require support through encouragement to join clubs, buddy systems, Circle of Friends, development of understanding of the nature of Down's syndrome.
- Effective parent partnership is essential for the pupil to settle into a new school and good communication is important for joint strategies to take place.
- Homework will need to be recorded in a diary and the amount given may need to be reduced in quantity.

Further information can be gained from the Down's Syndrome Association: Transition from Primary School to Secondary School. Alternative Accreditation at Key Stage 4.

Individual Education Plans

The following pen pictures describe pupils of different ages and are followed by examples of Individual Education Plans which aim to address the key issues.

Leanne

Leanne is a four year old who is in a school nursery. Her receptive language is much better than her expressive language, she is developing these skills by using signing. She prefers adult company and does not choose to play with her peers. Leanne is not yet hand dominant and uses an immature palmar grasp when making marks on paper. She finds it difficult to hold and place scissors appropriately to cut. Leanne has learnt to go up and down the slide but lacks awareness of the danger of jumping from a height or the consequences of other children using equipment, riding bikes, playing on swings. Leanne is not yet toilet trained and has bowel problems which complicate the development of this.

Sara

Sara is a happy, sociable six-year-old girl who is a happy member of her class. She has a language delay, using only a small range of single words supplemented by gesture, facial expression and sign language to communicate. Sara has glue ear, has frequent ear infections and has been prescribed spectacles. She has a thyroid problem and has appointments with the dietician. Sara has a poor concentration span and needs frequent changes of activity. She is resistant to adult-directed activities and can hit out. Sara has poor fine motor skills and uses an immature tripod grip to make attempts to write her name.

Tim

Tim is a ten-year-old boy who is sociable and popular in his class. He is very small for his age and tires easily. He has Hirschsprung's Disease, which causes occasional soiling problems and necessitates special toilet arrangements. He has glue ear and a fluctuating hearing loss. He has a severe speech and language difficulty, which affects the intelligibility of his speech; he understands Makaton signs but prefers not to use this form of communication. He wears glasses as he is long sighted (astigmatism). Tim has poor fine motor skills. He is working at the top of the P scales, towards level 1.

Mary

Mary is a petite, shy twelve year old who has very good language skills and is able to communicate easily, particularly with people with whom she is familiar. She has medical problems (a heart problem which has been resolved, stomach ulcers and rheumatoid arthritis) which cause frequent absences from school. The physical demands of a large secondary school, frequent class changes, the distances involved in movement around school, carrying equipment, can be very tiring. Mary is also very strong-willed and is not averse to absenting herself from lessons. Mary has to work hard to maintain friendship groups because of frequent absences.

School

Statement of special educational needs – band 2

Name: Leanne
Date: 13. 1. 04

Date of birth: 4. 1. 00
Review Date: 25. 3. 04

Nature of pupil's difficulties: Lack of expressive language skills. Not toilet trained. Poor fine motor skills.

Targets	Strategies	Resources	Evaluation
To use sign/words in group time.	Advice from SALT. Mirroring adult models for words/signs linked to group times.	Use of IT; Karaoke machine, tape recorder.	
	Using words/signs at group times when making choices for drinks, activities. Turn taking games with other children.	Card games with foods, toys to encourage using words/signs.	
To improve fine motor skills: to make vertical and horizontal marks in any media, to snip with scissors.	Making vertical horizontal arm movements. Pushing cars along tracks. Painting on large pieces of paper. Overwriting patterns with sticks or fingers in different media. Tearing paper, pre-scissors skills activities, using tongs.	Big paintbrushes, road track mat and small cars. Felt tip pens, chunky crayons. Lentils, sand, shaving foam, finger paint. Tissue paper. Specialist scissors, card.	
To develop toilet routines.	Visiting the toilet when other children go. Visual prompts to develop routines.	Trainer pants. Visual timetable plus visual prompts.	

Parental involvement: Leanne to start to wear pull-ups in school. To use the same visual timetable at home to encourage toileting routines. Encourage verbal/signed responses at meal times.

School

School action plus

Name: Sara
Date: 1. 1. 04

Date of birth: 1. 5. 97
Review Date: 24. 03. 04

Nature of pupil's difficulties: Resisting adult-directed activities. Lack of understanding of the relationship between the written and spoken word. Poor fine motor skills.

Targets	Strategies	Resources	Evaluation
To overwrite her name.	Making name with wooden letters. Making letter shapes in the air. Multi-sensory approach; overwriting writing letters in sand, foam. Walking round large letters made with a skipping rope, whilst articulating the correct formation. Using a variety of media.	Sand, shaving foam. Skipping rope. Chalks, large felt tip pens, large paintbrushes and newspaper.	
To use signs to indicate word recognition (5 family member names, Mum, Dad, Gran, cat, dog).	Learn signs for words. Matching words to words. Matching words to pictures using sign and word simultaneously.	Matching word games, e.g. Lotto games (played with another child). Photographs in a handmade book with words which can be matched by attaching with Velcro. Digital camera.	
To develop a more appropriate response to an adult request, i.e. moving to another activity.	Indicate expected activities using a visual timetable. One minute warning given of a change of activity. Modelling of appropriate behaviour. Photographs to prompt desired behaviour. Praise and reward system.	Visual timetable composed of photographs. Digital camera. Stickers, stamps, etc., as rewards, given directly after appropriate response is given.	

Parental involvement: Encourage Sara to practise pencil skills at home using dot-to-dot books, colouring books. Contribute to photograph collection, reinforce learning of words at home.

School

School action plus

Name: Tim
Date: 1. 5. 04

Date of birth: 2. 7. 93
Review Date: 18. 7. 04

Nature of pupil's difficulties: Poor recording skills. Hirschsprung's disease – doesn't go to the toilet and soiling results. Finding it difficult to develop understanding of value of money. Poor intelligibility of speech.

Targets	Strategies	Resources	Evaluation
To record ideas.	Use of prompts to enable Tim to produce ideas. Use of pictures, objects to help word retrieval. Alternative methods of recording ideas.	Home/school diary with comments/pictures about activities which have taken place at home. Pictures taken on school visits, of activities which have taken place in school, e.g. science experiments, baking activities. Clicker 4 with appropriate words installed. Tape recorder.	
To go to the toilet when necessary.	Develop toilet routines using visual prompts.	Visual timetable with pictures showing times to visit the toilet. CSA support to prompt this initially. Praise/rewards for carrying this out. Praise for asking to go to the toilet (indicated by holding up a card).	
To develop an understanding of the value of 1p, 2p, 5p and 10p coins.	Use of worksheets, ICT programs. Helping to collect tuck money with peer support. Taking a lead in 'playing shop' in the Nursery. Shop activities as part of Maths lesson.	Real coins. Cash till, shopping items.	
To encourage clear speech production when passing a message.	Reading messages, written in conjunction with CSA during the school day, to parents. Taking written messages to another teacher, which Tim reads out. Reading book to peers. Asking written questions on questionnaire for data collection.	Home/school diary. Staff to give opportunities in other classes. Compilation of questionnaires in Maths, Science lessons.	

Parental involvement: Contributions to home/school diary. Continue use of visual timetable at home to prompt visiting the toilet at appropriate times. Shopping with parents, giving opportunities to buy sweets of small denominations.

School

School action plus

Name: Mary
Date: 12. 4. 04

Date of birth: 19. 5. 91
Review Date: 6. 7. 04

Nature of pupil's difficulties: Difficulty maintaining friendships due to frequent absences from school. Poor organisation of movement around school to avoid fatigue. Absenting herself from certain lessons.

Targets	Strategies	Resources	Evaluation
To maintain friendships during absence.	Use of IT. Circle of friends who are encouraged to keep in touch with Mary. On-going 'buddy' system organised by older pupils.	Mobile phone, access to internet. Copies of lesson notes, news letters to be passed on.	
To attend lessons.	Timetables. Incentive to arrive at lessons.	A variety of sizes of timetables available. Peer pressure, class rewards – less homework, early lesson finish. CSA support in lessons she is finding difficult. Home/school links.	
To reduce fatigue.	Use of a locker/drop off point to reduce amount of equipment carried. Registration room on ground floor. Minimum amount of equipment to be carried around. Spare set of books to be kept in the subject rooms. Access to drink/snack.	Key attached to trouser pocket for locker. PE equipment to be left in a safe place. Addressing timetabling issues. Timetable and equipment needed to be checked with parents and only essential items to be brought. Spare set of books for each subject. Water towers, dried fruit available.	

Parental involvement: Parents to provide mobile phone, encouragement to keep in touch with friends. Parents to support timetabling and equipment organisation.

School

School action plus

Name:

Date:

Date of birth:

Review Date:

Nature of pupil's difficulties:

Targets	Strategies	Resources	Evaluation

Parental involvement:

Acknowledgements and useful contacts

Down's Syndrome Educational Trust (Down's Ed)
The Sarah Duffen Centre
Belmont Street
Southsea
Hampshire PO5 1NA
Tel: 01705 824 261

Including all children in the literacy hour and daily mathematics lesson
Department for Education and Skills
DfES 0465/2002

Jolly Phonics
Jolly Learning Ltd
www.jollylearning.co.uk

Kingston upon Hull Target Setting book
Learning Services
Essex House
Manor Road
Kingston upon Hull HU1 1YD
Tel: 01482 613423

Write from the Start
Ion Teodorescu and Lois Addy
LDA
Duke Street
Wisbech
Cambs PE13 2AC
Tel: 01945 46344
www.instructionalfair.co.uk

Nottingham Rehab Supplies
Findell Educational Ltd
Findel House
Excelsior Road
Ashby Park
Ashby de la Zouch
Leicester LE65 1NG
Tel: 0845 1204522

Number games/Trackerballs

Ready for writing
SEMERC
Granada Learning Ltd
Granada Television
Quay Street
Manchester M60 9EA
www.semerc.com

Starspell 2001
Down's Ed
(see above)

Writing with Symbols
Widgit Software1
102 Radford Road
Leamington Spa CV1 1IF
email literacy@widgit.com

Special Olympics
18 Grosvenor Gardens
London SW1 0DH
Tel: 020 7824 7800

Some literature, which is available from the Down's Syndrome Association:

Sandy Alton, Down's syndrome: your questions answered
The Early Years – Starting School
Sandy Alton, Children with Down's syndrome – Reading
Sandy Alton, Children with Down's syndrome – Behaviour
£1.50 each

Education Support Pack for Schools – Mainstream: Primary and Secondary
(UK Education Consortium for Pupils with Down's Syndrome, 2002)
£9.99

Sandy Alton, Including Pupils with Down's syndrome: Primary
(DSA and Scottish DSA)
First copy free

Further reading and specialist advice is available from:
The Down's Syndrome Association
155 Mitcham Rd
London SW17 9PG
Tel: 020 8682 4001
e-mail: info@downs-syndrome.org.uk
web site: www.downs-syndrome.org.uk

Issues for consideration

Issues to be considered by the senior management when including a pupil with Down's syndrome

Issue	✓	✗	Action
Is the governing body aware of the pupils with special educational needs and its responsibilities in ensuring that the needs of these pupils are being met?			
Are the buildings and furniture accessible to all pupils?			
Is there any additional adult support for the pupil with Down's syndrome?			
Are all staff given time to train and update skills to meet the particular needs of the pupil with Down's syndrome, e.g. signing, ICT?			
Are there methods of ensuring effective communication between home and school?			
What other agencies are involved in meeting the needs of the pupil and is time given to meet with outside agencies?			
Is time given to discuss the changing needs of the pupil?			
Are staff aware of recent legislation, LEA/SEN policies?			
Are strategies in place to support a pupil's emotional well-being?			
Does the school have any necessary medical information for the pupil, e.g. heart problems, glue ear?			
How does the school promote positive images of the pupil and positive peer group relationships?			
Are appropriate teaching strategies in place?			
Are any additional resources/strategies required to support curriculum delivery and do staff know where to access these, e.g. step boxes to facilitate access, pencil grips, computer programs?			

Some professionals who may be involved with the pupil

Professional	Personnel and contact number
Educational Psychologist	
Special Educational Needs Support Service	
Educational Service for Physical Disability	
Speech and Language Therapist	
Visual Impairment Service	
Hearing Impairment Service	
School Nurse	
Physiotherapist	
Occupational Therapist	
Educational Welfare Officer	
Down's Paediatric Specialist Nurse	

Small steps approach to recording progress in reading

	Started	Achieved	Comments
Shows interest in books			
Turns several pages at once			
Turns one page at a time			
Points to a named picture			
Turns pages to find a named picture			
Finds a named book on request			
Will sit and share book with an adult for an increasing amount of time			
Will sit in a small group to share a book			
Indicates what comes next in a repetitive story			
Matches objects to pictures			
Matches pictures to pictures			
Participates in a group lotto game			
Finds a name card when identified by a picture and name			
Matches name card to a corresponding name card from a selection of two			
Matches letters on a board game			
Matches words on a board game			
Finds a word amongst an increasing number of words			
Reads flash card words			
Reads words in books			

Name: ....

Small steps approach to recording progress in scissor skills

	Started	Achieved	Comments
Can crumple tissue paper			
Can tear tissue paper			
Can open and close scissors*			
Can snip with scissors with an adult to guide the movement			
Can snip without adult support			
Can snip to make a fringe			
Can cut a piece of card in two with an adult holding the card			
Can cut across a piece of card without help			
Can cut between two lines (reduce gap)			
Can cut along a broad felt tip line			
Can cut along a fine line			
Can cut between two lines which gently wave, build up the curves			
Can cut round a circle with concentric guidelines			
Can cut round a circle which has a broad felt tip outline			
Can cut round a square with broad parallel lines			
Can cut round a square with a thin outline			
Can cut out a variety of shapes			

*Can use trainer scissors or normal scissors. Card is easier to use than paper.

Name: ....